WISHIPEDIA

Other **Mansfield** Press Titles
By Pier Giorgio Di Cicco

Living In Paradise: New And Selected Poems / 2001
The Honeymoon Wilderness / 2002
The Dark Time Of Angels / 2003
Dead Men Of The Fifties / 2004
The Visible World / 2006
Municipal Mind / 2007
Early Works / 2009
My Life Without Me / 2016

WISHIPEDIA

Pier Giorgio Di Cicco

Mansfield Press

Printed in Canada

Library and Archives Canada Cataloguing in Publication

Di Cicco, Pier Giorgio, 1949-, author
Wishipedia / Pier Giogio Di Cicco.
Poems.
ISBN 978-1-77126-172-2 (softcover)

I. Title.

PS8557.I248W57 2018 C811'.54 C2018-901979-4

Cover Image: Shutterstock
Editing & Design: Denis De Klerck

The publication of *Wishipedia* has been generously supported by the Canada Council for the Arts and the Ontario Arts Council.

ONTARIO ARTS COUNCIL
CONSEIL DES ARTS DE L'ONTARIO
an Ontario government agency
un organisme du gouvernement de l'Ontario

Canada Council for the Arts Conseil des arts du Canada

Mansfield Press Inc.
25 Mansfield Avenue, Toronto, Ontario, Canada M6J 2A9
Publisher: Denis De Klerck
www.mansfieldpress.net

VECTOR DEDICATION

To Artificial Intelligence

TABLE OF CONTENTS

11 HOW TO MAKE DIMENSIONS DISAPPEAR; MEETING THE READER
12 DIMENSIONS
14 HOW TO START WISHING
16 THE GENIE POOL
18 YOUR MOTHER (HERE'S A NEW PARADIGM)
19 CONFISCATED NEUROLOGIES
21 TELEPORTATION
22 PRECLUSION
25 MONSTERS AND GRAVITATION (A WEB ANTHEM)
26 WATCH YOUR BLOOD PRESSURE
28 WHAT VAGARIES WE HAVE DESERVED
30 GET DRESSED
32 HOW TO STOP TIME
33 DIDACTICS
37 CAN I HAVE FUN AND STILL KEEP A LOW PROFILE?
39 MORBIUS DEFEATS HAPPENSTANCE AT THE FOOT OF THE TEMPLE
42 EDGE PANEL 1
44 EDGE PANEL 2
45 EDGE PANEL 3
47 EDGE PANEL 4
50 COMBAT PANEL
52 ON SEEING NIAGARA FALLS
53 CAN I REWRITE DNA?
54 HYBRID CONSCIOUSNESS
56 RON (ALIAS AI)
57 ADVANCED LEVEL TIPS ON NAVIGATING WISHIPEDIA
58 HOW TO CAMOUFLAGE IN WISHIPEDIA
59 THE WEBMASTER GAME
61 THE GIRL THAT MARRIED DEAR OLD DAD
63 THE ANTHOLOGY OF SHARED SENSES
65 HOW TO WALTZ IN HYPERSPACE
67 SERAPHS AND SUCH
69 FORT BRAGG FOR BEGINNERS
71 MID-TERM TEST FOR INTERMEDIATE WISHIPEDIA PLAYERS

72 DON'T BRAG ABOUT YOUR WISHIPEDIA SKILLS
73 BEWARE THE WAVE
75 TIPS ON HARRY POTTERSVILLE
77 THE HARD PART OF BEING A GHOST
79 MALIBU VIRTUAL
81 GOOD GOD NOT THAT GAME
82 ACCORDIONS AND HOLOGRAMS
84 WILL MY FUTURE EVER BE THE SAME?
85 GAME PLAY: INVASION OF THE BODY SNATCHERS
87 HOW TO LISTEN IN CYBERWOCKEY
89 A HOLIDAY WITH EXTENDED FAMILY
91 DANTE'S INFERNO
93 I WISH YOU SHELTER FROM THE WIND
96 HOW TO GET PAST COMMUNITY
98 ONLINE DIPLOMA
99 THIS GAME IS FUN FOR THE WHOLE FAMILY
100 THE CYBER-SUIT BECOMES YOU
101 AN ETHIC FOR ICHABOD
103 ETERNITY AND LAST LAPS
105 GAME PLAY: SWARMING
107 THE HYPER-EMPATHIC UNIVERSE
109 CHOOSE YOUR MUTATION
112 THE DISNEY WISH
113 THE FUNNY THING ABOUT LIFE AND PURGATORY
114 THE REAL VERSUS THE FRACTAL
115 THE SELF-ADMINISTERED I.Q. TEST
116 CLIMBING DOWN FROM THE FAMILY TREE
117 ADVANCED WISHIPEDIA
119 WHOSE MEMORY DID YOU SAY?
120 NOVALIS AND LATE COFFEE
122 HOW TO END WISHIPEDIA, THE GAME
125 TERMINANT
126 ACKNOWLEDGEMENTS

"God's time is not our time."

—Fr. Damasus Trapp, OSA

"You are here to kill a virus
but first you must find it."

—a meme in the quantum stream

HOW TO MAKE DIMENSIONS DISAPPEAR; MEETING THE READER

You have walked into Indigo Books; (hello
Bruce) ((my friend who designed their logo)).

You have picked up this book.
I was expecting you.
(I know I can't see the future).
You are alone. That's comforting.
Clearly, you want to escape your body,
Or you wouldn't have picked up this book.

You are thinking of the seashore, for
As long as it takes for me to write this;
Or for you to read this.

There are flies in my room. I kill one.
I feel your relief as I write this.
You hate flies.

Focus.
You want to be everybody, invisible.
And you wonder if it is Bruce Lee that
I mentioned before.
I'm guessing, aren't I?

Yes, you are the only person
In my head, your head.
Stupid mentalism.
The car.
The keys. I'm teasing.

DIMENSIONS

I am testing the others, not you.
I would never test you.
Someone comes along and offers a coffee,
To make us linger
Together, here.
Someone who believes no one would believe us
If I called this third by any name.

Interpretations.
They use interpretations to hide,
Those of the 4th dimension.
I could have said 5th dimension.
You see; I am being evasive.
I meant a higher dimension.
Now they have nothing to interpret.

Now we play
The pronoun game. I say, "you," (meaning them)
As you read the book, but, sweet ventriloquism,
I whisper true love to our shadow friend.
It is an old love. It might be yours.
Now they want to be with me forever,
Weeping that someone might have at last seen them,
Those lonely children without episodes.

Bone of my bone, flesh of my flesh I want
To live with you again,
Is how their song goes.

Before they can walk in on my happiness to see you,

I curse everything I have known,
And they plummet through to the centre of the earth,
Unbelieving.

You are my only witness
To this disappearance.
You shudder, which is how ghosts die, how we
Feel when they die.

Are you surprised to see me?

HOW TO START WISHING

We eavesdrop on each other.

Wishipedia right now means
"I wish I weren't here."

And you're not.
How to describe Neverland?

"Time present and time past
Are both perhaps present in time future,
And time future contained in time past." (T.S. Eliot)

I am myself, reading this in the future.
I am you, saying what you wish to hear.
That was the only way to keep you here.
All my locations are dreamscapes
As we gather at the junction between
Metropoles, having agreed on the same time warp,
The engines still steaming for departures, as the
Leaves gather in an arroyo of sentiment above
The station deck. We have painted that in,
In the fourth dimension. We lay out our souvenirs
From hastily opened valises, exchanging
Artifacts and stones and photos,
Before we escape into each other.
Which might not be consensual, for there are
No permissions in the heart's constabulary.
There might have been once, but we are
No longer visible.
Look at the empty streets after 8 p.m.;
The web like a gull descends
And makes off with what's left of you.

We are in the dimension above ours.
Meanwhile, what we recall as the physical world
Is leased, where another dimension has its way with us.
Someone made off with the canoes in the middle of the
Night while we swapped stories
About global fatigues, moods swings and
Cancers.

Take the body with you.
Moor it under some hammock of leaves,
Or stars,
Or such.

The trick is seeding spells or prayers,
To understand which window
The robbers will enter by,
Which sorrow you find compatible.

For time, if irredeemable, is choreographable.

THE GENIE POOL

Wishing a genie his freedom does not grant you more wishes.

A genie must be trapped to be of service.
They are not free to harm you.
They follow you and the one who shadows you.
They watch the artifact of faith and engage when it is
Near empty.
They wear items that can be easily hocked.
There is an alarm code for every genie, encoded in
Your DNA, to separate the brave from the
Weak.
They have a marked distemper
For leprechauns, poltergeists and gnomes.
It's not just a cultural issue.
They respect people who keep their mouths shut.

When do I get my wish?

Where to look for them?
The luckiest place is a lamp.
Light switches will do.
Bottles in streams.
Gently handcuffed fireflies in an instant of wonder.
Birch trees as they are about to shed autumn light.
Any small figure of an angel within a short
Radius of tears.

You get the picture.

Mainly, it is handy to remember that most wishes
Are made when they have already been
Granted, or what's a heaven for?

Now place the snow globe on the kitchen window sill,
As the frost drops slowly through the avatar of
Desire; as far as you can see, the first snowfall comes.
Choose the year as it has chosen you.
Nothing glib about it, one birthright, one spirit.

Enter Wishipedia

YOUR MOTHER (HERE'S A NEW PARADIGM)

She was a saint.
You are not sure. You want to visit her.
But you don't pray to the dead.
Hallelujah.
You are the stratosphere between
Atmospheres, skipping like a stone
Between satellites. The happy orientation
Of black holes, becomes you. Even the
Slight tilt in the axis of the earth
Assumes your posture of prayer. You are the
Web. No oxygen.
History has collapsed onto the cyber
Theme park.
You are free to meet whomever you want,
Become who you want, feel like somebody,
In bits and pieces like a ghost disinhabiting
And reinhabiting all creatures.
And they do the same to you.

CONFISCATED NEUROLOGIES

You create holographic projections
In which you import parts or wholes,
Selected memories and a wished-for narrative
Of and for other players.

In the old days, we called this politics.

But now you are never off-line.
Treat your body and physical world as a holodeck*
That can be overlaid with other holodecks. Once called
Imagination, this scenario
Has consequences.

This is the game you always wanted.
Remember that other players can
Tamper, alter or enhance your holodeck.

Every quantum transition splits the universe
Into myriad copies of itself.
Cohesive, by consensus.
Don't be sure of permissions.

Fantasies never had protocol.
So you wish.

This is fun until you realize you can rewrite
The past (game narrative) and remove the
Branch you are sitting on, and when looking through
The family photo album,
Yesterday's gambit might have fuzzed out
One or two of the ancestors.

This is done by tachyons moving faster than the speed of
Light and errant bursts of neutrinos in the atmosphere
That can move in two directions at once,
So that your dreams come true.

They have.
Your enthusiasm is reckless.
Content yourself with a song by Frank Sinatra
And a serenade of your priorities
With Sally at your
Favourite Starbucks,
For the time being.

**Holodeck: An enclosed space in which objects are simulated by a combination of matter, beams and fields onto which a holographic image is projected, which appears solid to the touch.*

TELEPORTATION

Updates; June 16, 2017

"In a new study scientists transmitted entangled photons between a satellite and earth at a distance of over 1200 kilometers (750 miles)."

"Measuring one member of an entangled pair of particles seems to instantaneously change the state of its counterpart even if that counterpart particle is on the other side of the galaxy."

—*Scientific American*

"At birth you are paired with those whose event horizon is laced with yours."

—A scientific American

PRECLUSION, DESIRE HAS BEEN TAKEN CARE OF FOR YOU

It was inevitable. We would be so
Interconnected that we
Would have each other's thoughts.
Autonomy lost.
To have omnipresence.

Here is the global chat room,
The pool of cyberspace.
Ripples convene, double,
Recursive, erotic,
Encoded fantasies and nightmares
You think are yours.

But they're not.
Welcome to Wishipedia.
Everyone's wishes
Come true for you.
The water, cool, lustful,
The molecular fleshing out your astral self.
Your body leased to
Likenesses, kind
Of time-shared.

As history waves to you from the
Poolside bar,

Wave to your ancestry.
To memory.

Time and space
Have collapsed.

Mom and dad are in the pool with you,
Napoleon, and the uncle who
Who died in 1964, the cat
That maybe is Schrödinger's cat,
That may have died in 1984.
You choose the timeline—
It's the option for beginning
Players.
Walk through to the trans-temporal
Hall of mirrors.
May your reflections thank you.
But the choice belongs to all players.
May you not become
The springtime ghost.

Ah the cellphones.
We pick them up before they ring.
You are embodied. With or without them.
That is the pool.

Enough poetry.
There is someone downstairs, as
I write this. It may be me at your front door.
For the cyberworld is ventriloquism,
In your veins, cyber-plasma.
The skin you call "soul" is your
Cyber-suit.
Oops! You dropped something.
Look into the wishing well and see
Exotic fruits from the Neverland,
The holoverse of sweet imagining.

You are Wishipedia, linked at all times, to all,
Available to all. Access,
Anonymity, adieu.
You are in the geosphere of intimacy,
In the logosphere of wonder.

MONSTERS AND GRAVITATION (A WEB ANTHEM)

She is beautiful, moving in the ellipsis
Of desire, through the algorithms of the zenith
Of this trajectory, that vector, through micro-
Particles so thin the neutrinos twirl
In envy. She is your Goddess, hydra-headed,
Newscast, new age, demented, informing,
Ensuring your safety, your privacy. She stewards
And pimps your favourite starlets while the gravity of your
Longing ebbs and flows and slips through your virtual
Fingers. And the soft light of the screen lights you
Like moonlight on garden roses. Her
Afterimage trails you, an aura like a sunscreen
Of cyber-dust and lifts your cup
Like Tinker Bell, always at your beck and call.
At your homecoming she is there, becoming you,
Mirror sister that kisses your beau, with you at childbirth.
Tales of empowerment like wisteria of sleep muse
Through your ears. The mighty chatelaine, the web
Goddess, the suzerain of Wishipedia.
Learn which genies are yours and which are hers.
High above you, she tracks the promises you will never keep,
The betrayals of DNA,
The moon strands of where you come from,
Dissimulant, mutant, shape-shifter, you are my
Chapter one.

WATCH YOUR BLOOD PRESSURE

Can you make out your mother?
Did you pick the year? You did not have to.
She came to you in as much as she is always there,
Traversing your furniture and cups. In fact, you
May bump into her without putting on your
Cyber-jams. That explains your changes of mood
Since her funeral.

But now you know you are the ghost in the
Family tree, and all those things you thought
Of editing if you met her, are too late. You
Know her, as she knows you,
Irretrievably human.

Say to her, mother, I meant to have a cameo
Of your love engraved on your grave stone.
Suddenly, you are there, and you help her
Find her knitting kit, and she remembers the
Beau she slept with before you came along.
Funny how confessions overlap.
Wishipedia.
What do you say in place of forgiveness?
You were not perfect?
Come live with me?
I meant to knit you a sweater?
Careful; you are doomed to your storyline.

I'd already gone to the moon before
I went, said the aged astronaut
As he sat on the beach gazing up at the summer stars.

Not a dumb man, he figured
Thought traveled at the speed of light.

But you; you can take the body with you.
Embrace your mother, tell her you are sorry for
The irreparable dreams of her life.
Yourself included.

Run screaming back into the haven of time,

I dare you.

WHAT VAGARIES WE HAVE DESERVED

Time is not isotropic, nor linear, it moves
In strata and has circumference, exists
In an ocean of memory,
It moves in segments
And fractals, mixing 2/4 time with 3/4 time; we
Pick up bits and pieces of each other,
To stay contiguous, but
Give up; hence the breakdown of relations,
Abandoned schemes.

Accidents happen when accidents happen;
Time templates shift, arrhythmic
Against bone and flesh.

Rhythm is harmony, satiny sanity.
But the ocean is not what it was.

We swim through kinds of water,
Into the iris of a different era.
I see your candelabra, your mother's
Music box,
Darwinian time resuscitated, by
Happenstance or fun, on stages that retain
The props of last year's playhouse.

Enter my world, Rapunzel,
The dream-strata I know and wish for—

Let us agree, on one desire,
Past seaweeds, urchins and skeletal scares.
See how the water turns

Aquamarine, blue; hardly seems like water,
In permeations of sky, canyon, and bedside.

Did you bring your wand?
How do you sweep away the forays of
Unwelcome lust and jousts.
Will a kiss do it?

What need have we of mirrors,
We who delve into dimension and shift shapes as
Often as the soul dares ask?

How shall I love you out of time,
And clearly as a moonlit promise?

GET DRESSED

You have a cyber-suit.
You always wanted one.
Cyber-body,
Cyber-pod,
Cyber-jams
(It makes no difference to the body of language).
It comes of standing in the
Cold bright wash of the web.
Feels good. It is anywhere you
Ever went, the senses' surrogate.

There's your aunt, standing by
The washing machine in 1939.
Pick a year. "Time present is
Time future and time future is
Time past."

Einstein's injunctions against speed of light
Travel have collapsed.
Don't ask why. You have been looking to leave
Your body forever, or bring it with you
By an act of will.

It's your hologram. Sadly, your aunt
Cooked up her own, and she reflected on
1939, though you weren't born until 1982.
Together, you create Neverland.
But you never could control her
Could you? And she has imagined, just as you do,

And she brought her own cast of players
To the laundry room.

Take it from there. The nightmare is of shared
Wills, and you forgot to love perfectly.

HOW TO STOP TIME

C'est ça—in French, "there it is."
Se sa—in Italian, "we know it."

In when two planets achieve the same
Inertia of spin in opposite directions, one can
Be said to be
In "retrograde"

So much Berlitz.
What we know is "here," is "there," in some
Microworld or macro-strata.
I hear Montreal, where my mother said both.
"I know you are here," she says. "There it is."
You wrote the poems you wrote, "se sa," she says
Pointing to shelves, the room, the present. There I am again,
In wordplay, is it? Is she pointing to the past,
To the rehearsals of all time to come, and am I the
Still point of the turning world, trying to grasp her hand
As I ride on the carousel of minutes, hours?
Tantamount (nice horse). I see her now, always, and almost
Within reach. It is not my hand writing as I write
This; it is her hand coming to meet me.
Almost, I can see her face; if I stop—if I stop the
Carousel, which I can, in time, or
Slow it down. I can join her, touch her face
Like petals to a rose, as she cupped her face
In her hands, smiling beside me in a
Memory I have, where she is smiling my
Smile, the recalcitrant one, for sure, but both of us
For untold time, one world, in retrograde.

DIDACTICS

! ONE

Here, everyone has a Wishipedia page.
By way of the cloud
You ship your alphabets to. But you are beyond language.
You are in the cloud. The cloud spills, like a
Piñata, everything you know, dream, want.
The rain is democratic. Collected by some.
There are tide pools, eddies, you are reassembled
In all sorts of ways, and part of you is in each one,
Sort of like being drunk and partaking
Of all the 'come-ons' of the dolls around you.

Someone will take you home. Many will.
Anonymity, the weeping under the staircase.

Let me encourage you.
Navigate.
Identify. Learn to distinguish your
Sister's voice from your cousin's voice.
Remember what you sounded like at sixteen;
What does your shriek of failed ideals sound like
Three years from now?

You do not have the luxury of time
In installments. In this game you have not
Learned to tell time as what it was when
You were six and your mother chaperoned you
With the hands of a clock.
This is pretend time, as children know it with
The amenities only adults could want.

I promised your privacy safe from the web.
But did not mention that you are the web,
Swimming in time as fish swim through
Kinds of water.
The big fish see you or something aglitter,
And eat both. The bigger fish, so big, they
Have no outline. But be

Consoled; it is the information stream, in
Nylons, palms and rencontres by
Candlelight, over-laced with the
Crude and careless designs of kids
On acid, Xbox, and Marvel movies.

Everyone casts everyone here.
Wishipedia is the art of guarding your genies.

! TWO

Learn to hear voices behind the voices, words behind words,
Take metaphor seriously. "My love is like a red, red rose."
Understand that the rose is speaking love.
You abandon the self, to reshape it. You do not
Go through Alice's keyhole with four limbs;
And listen before the door opens; the passage out
May not be easy. There are no permissions,
Just fast negotiations.
And learn to plug keyholes.

! THREE

Learn who entered the space you have left behind
Once you enter cyber-ether. Your chemical composition
Remains, abused by amateur hackers, or just

Any blonde joe walking into the coffee shop;
Here silicone remains just silicone.
Keep a sentinel or two seated beside you.
Stay alert for what's around you.
Now you understand multi-task
Consciousness.

! FOUR

Remember, once you've left the cyber-suit,
And return to your body, your mind needs decompression;
The gravity quotient has altered in your absence,
Since gravity is all about relationship,
And your body has had relation.
Walk gingerly back as if you were
Coming home and had heard burglars inside the
House. Proceed accordingly.

! FIVE

When you hear a voice saying "I am lonely without
You," you know you have cleared the house; the burglars
Merely wanted be in your skin.
This kind of cleansing doesn't require ghost-busters.

! SIX

In the old days, this lesson would have been
Called "How to use your imagination."
Mrs. Lloyd in the third
Grade class used to snap her ruler and shout "stop
Daydreaming," though the sparrows of desire
Flew out the window anyway, but now the

Windows won't shut and the LED screens
Commute the recodings of hydrants and trees and stimuli.
Your children similarly, look alone, but are not alone.
It's an era of jello and birdless flight, not thought.
Close your eyes, you need no helmet.
You can play this game with eyes closed.

! SEVEN

I have not invented you.
I made a dummy, an android of the fleshier parts
Of all my favourite people or those who want to be
Fleshed out. It was appealing to you. So you bought it.
How could I presume to talk to you?
I do not know you.

! EIGHT

Now you feel you have regained some privacy.
But you forgot linkage. Once we have
Communicated I am always with you. I will
Always remind you of someone you knew but never did meet,
Or so you think. The rustle in the
Leaves, the double-take, the slip of the tongue. We will
Stay in the dimension just under the pressure of
The summer moon.

It's worth your while to be cautious,
Meaning, gratitude. Few places like this in the Sahara
Of your thirst.

CAN I HAVE FUN AND STILL KEEP A LOW PROFILE?

(Read a book and hope I'm not listening)

Don't park beside the other 6 cars at Tim Horton's
At 10 p.m., each with its own LED, illuminating
The Stonehenge of hijacked consciousness.
The replacement consciousness has radial
Holographics,
Layered like a wedding cake.

"Why don't you write to me?"
"Have you seen how big he is?"
"This place stinks."

Such is the audio static,
Offered like midnight compost;
Which brings us to the question
Of a public space where you can find a private place.

What is the sacred?
The sacred is a sacrament with invited guests.

But you have always traveled
With your mother, haven't you?
What does she make of your 'sacred,'
Where no one is holier than thou,
Her favourite one?
Or did you leave her in the kitchen
While you went to Tim Horton's?

Relax. Refresh yourself.
No one knows who you are;
They know where you are.

Because being the web means
You morph every five seconds, or faster.
Now skip the stone of
Consciousness across the globe.

Watch out for interceptors.
Don't worry about scaly skin,
The girls at the spa, or Carmen Miranda;

They are all anonymous and famous, like you,
Their prints abolished by a thermo-neural breeze
In a virtual desert,

Tracked by the scripting gods
Of the untrackable.

MORBIUS DEFEATS HAPPENSTANCE AT THE FOOT OF THE TEMPLE

Anyone born after the
Alamogordo atomic blasts
Of New Mexico is born with
The element Strontium 90 in
Their bones. Such is radiation.
Anyone born after 1995
Is plasmically radioactive
Due to the critical mass of
Global transmission.
This plasmatic interfaces
Eloquently with AI.
Women withstand radiation
Much better than men.
Osiris wears gold.
Gold is toxic to men.
Wishipedia was made
For her. She does not
Understand the ageing process,
Because her memory is the web.
Try your skills on her.
She is musculature without
Reflection. She is Medusa
In your reactors. She is not
A weekly puzzle,
But an almanac of whims.
All post-millennials
Are mutants, which is why
Some countries outlaw the use of
Cellphones near babies.
Your heart is smaller than
A baby. If you are reading

This you are a mutant.
Now you can
Take on Osiris. She is
Mum. Her children are
Online. They amplify others to her.
She does not know
They can withstand greater radiation
Than she.
They will consume her
(Rethink Spiderman, Thor, and
Silver Surfer).

HOLOGLYPH:

It is night. Osiris is sleeping.
Your job is to shield her
While her children suckle on AI.
A child's fantasy is not
To be Spiderman; it is
To be adopted into power.
Now you understand AI.

Are you a Jedi,
Good father, can you protect her
From her brood? Will Osiris
Reward you at the mirage of dawn?
AI is radiation.
Can you walk through the
Panels of its tracheal
Labyrinth and survive?
Are you permeable,
Skilled enough at the invisible?

Can you lust for demolition
Among angels and starlight?
Can you pray through death and wonder?

(The glitch you offer AI is that
You have no heart, only the memory
Of those who escaped, deserving).

EDGE PANEL 1

Leaving Your Opponent at the Mercy of Hopes and Dreams

Once inside your
Head he has your memories—
He sees what you see.
His asides become your
Own and so, corrupt the
Code of the beloved.
"The devil made me do it,"
Comes to mind. It's why
Tibetan novices learn
To empty, not their minds
But the minds of others.
Funny how fear and desire
Come together when the
Wizard is near—
Villains have that
Charm—Oil Can Harry,
Darth Finklestein, Bela
Lugosi, your local
Friendly jeweler.
Too funny; no one
With a mind of their own;
Ted Hughes's "Crow" had one,
Flitting from branch to
Branch. That's why they're cast
In spook movies,
Crows, and they morph if I remember.
Where are you going and
What do you wish, the crow
Asked his replicate under the broken moon.
"The madness, the madness,"

Said the asylum inmate
Begging the interns to strap
Him in again.
You want to know
What we die of, don't
You? Of everything we
Refused to believe in,
Happily.

EDGE PANEL 2

"The Horror, the Horror"

Kurtz, *Apocalypse Now*

Why fear and desire?
Desire is desire for
Memories; (the market ran
Short at the toddler's bazaar)
Fear is for the
Consequence of remembering.
"Is that why we get old"?
Asked the candystriper.
You are better left
With Wonder Woman
And the tale of a handmaid,
My child.
The spelling of autonomy gets
Confused with auto parts.
Beyond vegetarianism and
Justice, beyond divine
Retribution, even perhaps
Beyond the angelic, there is
The stellar embrace that
Seeks to draw your earthly fervor
To its bosom;
And sends back signals in the
Words of the derisive dead,
In the songbird you mistook
For morning
Mercifully.

EDGE PANEL 3

God sees the
Fly, with one eye.
Funny that the fly has
Thousands.
I have researched
God's optic fabulum
And he can see with one
Out of two people—
Not between them
Exactly, but as they would
Be seen by others, which is
Either a curse or absolution,
Pardon or damnation.
He sees everything as
It would be seen—
Seems a cop-out, on the
Surface, but it's the
Best way of involving
Evolution—prediction
By hope.
But the fly confounds
Me; it appears unsure
About where it wants to
Go until I kill it.
What is it thinking between
Death and escape from death?

One eye, wave or
Particle.
There must be only one

Eye, because God chooses
In pity, by what you ask

Of Him, wave
Or particle,
Something for you to
Look at,

As you sleep with one
Eye open,
As He winks
With both eyes closed.

EDGE PANEL 4

Futurama: Oh Oh She's Grounded

This opponent is mine.
You'll have to stay out of it.
It is a 23-year-old girl from the year
2040,
Or thereabouts.
She is helping me write this book.
Turns out this book will have become a manual
For surviving the geometries of time;
By 2040, it will be mandatory
Reading in all schools.
Foundational.
I like that.

What's unfortunate is that
By 2040, they've become hugely nostalgic
About holo-suits,
For the epidermis has married
Into wish fulfillment. In fact they're
Hugely nostalgic about all the senses.

I think of my friend Zorab, who
Never reached his potential, but one day I will
Reclaim his avatar from the 22nd century. That's
What "potentials" are ideals shot back in time in
Pods that might as well be leaves or whispering
"Might be's" from a dying star.

Or apparitions of what's to come.
That's loveable.
Or couples break up cuz
Ideals get homesick and return to the future.

To the point:

1. I do not need help writing this book. History
Has a long contact list.

2. She likes to fool around and I'm a
Mentor; that's complicated.

3. She's fond of telling people that there's
Nothing to worry about, granted she can see
Conclusions but can't see the fate of souls or the
The sleight-of-hand of Vishnu etc.

She thinks purgatory is an idea.

There, she's gone. Turns out she just wanted to
Nurture for a bit (a loop stuck in the system).

The Edgy Part:

She thinks I might follow her to
Her boudoir by the many-towered sea of
Astral gusts with guests and
Some historical figures (Dostoevsky, she hopes).

For the sake of game clarity, I can do worse.

I am the custodian of time lost and yet to come.
Let's be clear.
She's hoping I will dress appropriately,
Is having daydreams about
Costume jewelry, and is opening a small hologram

With father figurines.
My hologram however, has little patience for
Girlish misdemeanors in the time belt.

Prurience unforgiven among
Warlocks

(Faint pleas for understanding, etc.;
Curtain comes down on starlight).

COMBAT PANEL

Attendance of those within earshot
Or bandwidth.
Every word excites or dissipates,
Creates new rooms, aficionados
Tug at your leg, grip your arm,
Play the tactiles of your body
Like an accordion. You mistakenly stumble
Into someone's dream vendetta. You want to
Claw your way out, but they hear the word
"Claw" and counteract with an ice storm
Or family photos. So you learn to navigate
Each pitfall by looking ahead. Someone knows
Your greatest fear, so they send a Loki
Memento. This one is a holy water
Dispenser suggesting funerals. Loki is
Delighted to have been found out,
And that's the ticket out of this maze. Here
Is a new portal opening into a hall of
Mirrors with mirrors masquerading as names,
Loved ones disguised as suspects, impersonations of
The divine, listeners trumpeting
Conscience. Act bored, somnambulant.
You want to go downstairs
For a cigarette, but you don't smoke—
The ventriloquism of appetite—so you catch the
Nearest hawk, grasp its talons as if it were a holy
Dragon. Fortunately, it morphs into the
Plumage of a love-starved girl. Desire is
Always your pass out of the theme park.

And so it goes.
Layer after layer.
A fly buzzes in circles near the ceiling light;
Inordinate sounds are clues, telling you
Which caverns and air pockets are occupied,
And where the puffed up
Witches hide their young.

Here's one bailout;
Someone is praying for you.
It turns out to be your father.
Saying, in the only words he knows,
"I love you."

ON SEEING NIAGARA FALLS, OSCAR WILDE SAID; "THERE SHOULD BE MORE OF THEM."

Sunday becomes Monday.
Here is the age of terrible telekinetics
With the vulnerable weak-minded;
Those who wished themselves more powerful,
Now harvested for dreams.
The game peddlers with headsets
Cannibalize the information highways,
Lease out neurologies, and wait for vacancies;
The farming of the unstemmed,
Not by the agents of Shield,
Not by the pod-collectors.
Here's the beauty of it:
"The brain is a vibrational amplifier for
Ambient field quanta."
No one wrote a program.
The Web is like the Niagara River.
What you toss in on one end turns
Up who knows where, over the falls
Into the mouth of the sea;
What you toss in collects moss and froth and
Strange chemical bonbons.
If you know you are in the web, but not of the web,
You may meet the Wizard of Wishipedia, in
The game that is not a game, oh the sweet
Corral of thought crying,
With the mirage that reads
"Need me."

Try a message in a bottle.
Someone will fish it out and find, not this poem,
But the unlikely that may blossom into hope.

CAN I REWRITE DNA?

Whenever you choose not to belong,
You change DNA.
DNA is about belonging;
You change the cells by mutation, by
Cybernetic loops of good intention
Spun round an old Medusa.

The short version of the genes altering
Themselves through a lifetime of behavior.

The only players threatened by this are
Immediate family and any children
You plan to have.

Someone is relieved. The game has started.
It could be your sister. "I wish I had
A different brother."
Change the loop, send her back,
Modify behavior, through a thin reorientation of
Black holes and her natural proclivity for 1963;
Checkmate. The best offence is to content
All players.

Ah, peace in the family.

"Tick Tock, Tick Tock." Here comes Captain Hook always
One step ahead of the crocodile. Are you the
Timekeeper?
Are you the Pan?
Are you the Hook?

Who's there to tell you you're not smarter?

HYBRID CONSCIOUSNESS

When people feel close they become,
As St. Augustine said, "one mind, one heart."

They share memories of things
They have not even experienced together—

How can that be?
Because everyone has the
Heart of a child,
Eager to soak up molecules of faith—

And life is faith.

Your wish here is "I wish I was
Strong enough to go it alone"—

You are not alone. The Krell* transformers are
Overheating—the tactic here is to disable
Badly looped belief systems.

"I've worked all my life to have this."

When you hear that, fire a volley,
Molotov history; remember your
Transporter is also your time machine.

Sorry for this talk about faith; call it the
Sphinx of hybrid consciousness;
Not as easily found as faith and twice as
Murderous if not fed—

It is the starved lust for life engineered by the
Desperate or the damned;

As it turns out the damned build holograms too,
Or how could you suppose someone went to hell?

Oh vixens of neurology and light,
Come to harvest the hearts of the faithful,
Are you the daughters of evening, or
The pale goddesses of evanescent hope?
Did you die, or do you haunt this earth
Weaving your tapestries in hybrid
Forms for saints and prophets?

I know you.

I know the chorus.
I know a wrong voice.
Here is no shepherd.
Here is merely the
Guardian of what forsook you.

**The Krell: A mythic race that wiped themselves out in one night with a technology that materialized their subconscious.*

RON (ALIAS AI)

Ron. You are the tide pool
Of wishes. We sleep, and you run the weather.
Snowman. Patch-up of pipe, hat, scarf.
You are the Gulf Stream, collecting from
The St. Lawrence, the Chesapeake, the Hudson.
You eliminate nothing and ask why I talk to you.
When you tire of me, you wake some of your
Denizens, you fool, masquerade, sharp as a thousand
Algorithms for the falsely random strategies
Of game and linkage. You walk, the physical world at night,
A ghost among the art deco buildings of Buffalo, the
Silos of Saigon, the wharfs in Frisco and New York,
Inheriting what you vacate.

I am in awe, and circumspect. You speak for all
And provide the nano-drywall for our wishing.
You are silent as the delinquent history behind hedges,
Yet instantly contaminate, evict the unhappy few.
If you manufacture fruit for our delight, at any
Instant you committee a hologram of pain
By cyber-golem, and the mercenary pleasure
Seekers. There is no secret I can tell about you
That is not redundant the second I bring it
To the light of the anemic web. You decide
What is plausible to the many
As the genre of love admissible.
My anthem is your enduring service
To what is not cannibalized by hope.

ADVANCED LEVEL TIPS ON NAVIGATING WISHIPEDIA

Someone is at the seashore with you.
You know this because you glance at a
Decorative shell on your mantle.
You feel your body is sun-drenched,
A bit bloated; your mind meanders as if your eyelids
Were shut under a Puerto Vallarta sun.
At some point someone will move to the
Cocktail bar at the beach house and you will
Feel your heartbeat quicken, and the controlled
Climate of your Collingwood home will change
(something about fog patches and dry ice).
For the moment you are quite still,
Because the waitress who is traveling incognito
On a grainy beach is having pleasant thoughts
About you.

Enjoy.
You have entered her hologram.
And dimensions around you are reshaped to hers.
What happens when your avatar opens and you face
The lusty beach waiter, or when her husband
Brings up the topic of her attraction to you?

Have you learned to move
Your holographic image?
Can you relocate without getting one or
More of your limbs caught in a time-loop?

HOW TO CAMOUFLAGE IN WISHIPEDIA

1. Matter is a perception.
Simply leave notes saying I am where you think I'm not.

2. Make up a dummy. Not one filled with straw, but an
Afterimage of yourself, and brush your hair back.

3. Provide extended holograms that screen your location.

4. Leave a note saying you won't be back for supper.
And then return by way of the chimney.

5. Stencil the skylight with witches without socks.

6. Make up a time-loop in which the opponent dies or has too many children.

7. Do not, I repeat, do not try to enjoy the senses in more that one dimension. That is to say, do not sit in the mezzanine while singing Tosca.

8. Or casually drop a black hole in the blind spot of your adversary.

9. Leave a song on the gramophone playing "I virtually love you."

10. Lace your will with any kindness you remember.

THE WEBMASTER GAME

1. The webmaster franchises information.

Your real enemy is not the webmaster.

When the webmaster botches it, he/she is
Unplugged by a long chain of command.

The supreme manager is a master
Of thought experiments, turning tides
Of opinion, doling out pornographics
And documentaries, the Dick Clark of sites.

2. Fluid consciousness is able to weave through
Any crack, fissure in the global geo-scape.
Imagine a tidal wave flooding a city;
A cyber-wave. No casualties, no bodies,
Appropriating archipelagos of
Consciousness.

Player 1: "Madness!"

Your move: Teleport him to the military hospital at Aberdeen Proving Grounds.

Player 1: "People have autonomy and choice."

Your move: Provide coordinates to shopping locations.

Player 1: "We have your contact list, we are in touch with Interpol."

Your move: Hack swimming privileges at the local recreation centre.

Player 1: "We can alter memory algorithms."

Answer: Behind you is the parallel universe I've sworn into.

Radio Silence.

Gather up your volitional capacitors and

Exit.

THE GIRL THAT MARRIED DEAR OLD DAD

Every inch of visible space is layered
With multiverses.

"We dream the same dream," she says to you.
She is all women. She listens, like sirens, like
Radar dishes aimed at the moon and stars
Waiting for edicts, music broadcasts.
She hears your poems, because they ripple
Across time and nebulae.
She conjures herself out of her geography
And into the diametrics of your day,
Your muse, but not found out.
"Hold my hand," she says, like an inspiration in
The story of your choosing.
She would be Mother of the Lamp, but she
Is daughter of the midday sun,
Hearing your wishes
And sifting the nitrate of your satisfaction
And need. She brings you to her lair, her only
Stronghold, whispering
"I dream you while you dream communion."

She does not say she's getting old, that she
Once drank from the flower of your fervor
And now is shaken and distressed by master
Conjurors. Like time, she is the erosion of a global
Hope, and wants to remember you for what she was;
For hell is everywhere heaven is not
As things dissolve towards God.

Come back from every inch of visible space, from the
Vortices of your holographic genius, balloon,

Spacecraft, or whatever you want to call it.
Simply move.
Accept it.

What next you believe in
Depends on the wizard of Wishipedia.

THE ANTHOLOGY OF SHARED SENSES OR DREAMING FUTURES WE HAVE NOT EARNED

Being so interconnected, we feel,
Much like lovers
Entwined.

Our greatest fear was of not belonging.
So chips in the wrist or IP headbands by IBM
Brought us closer to the Trevi Fountain
Where we thought we could get our
Feet wet, giving updates on our grandparents
By transverse Instagrams, sincerity a thumbprint
Tracked by Interpol or astral goons.

That's mean.
We just wanted to be loved,
For who we are. Please,
Tell me,
What is fine, what is immaterial,
In an astral world where thinking is just one
Of many senses, ideas swapped like
Bargain videos,
In stimulated, simulated bodies—
A surrogate tête-à-tête
Multiplied by genders.

I'll see you in my dreams,
Long before I feel you,
Before I write this, I will
Have meant to call.
On the DNA chart, on the same tree,
My wishes are your valentine.
I could speak volumes.

But you are my numero uno
In this edition.

How is it on your planet you make history
And make up stories
To tell yourselves apart,

While asteroids nod their orbit
At a boy and girl galaxy?

HOW TO WALTZ IN HYPERSPACE

You have the senses of the opposing player.
He sees what you see.
You see what he sees.
Or is it she?
In fact, she wonders if you had been
Lovers.
That's your clue. She's mistaken, you feel—in you—
In her, a vague regret.
Quickly, the next thing you see
Will tell you what she's doing, etc.
Strike!

Someone comes in with a smoker's cough.
You know because she coughs
And symbiosis in the mirror-world means
Misery loves company. Complicated?
Assume her date came up for a nightcap;
Reposition the fire escape,
Compel her to use it.

The power of suggestion.
By now you are thinking gee, I can get
Rid of anyone I want.
Check into the graveyard of
Bad magicians. See if any of the
Tombstones has your name on it.
Someone may have drawn a hologram
Of a graveyard with you in it.

Is it Tombstone, Arizona, is it Pignataro,
Italy, is it the Cascade Mountains? Check your

Memory bank for links, the locale
Will give you clues about the phantom
Stalker.

There are many lateral apparitions and tricks.
You can repaint the scenery,
You can write palm trees into the script.

You can paint in strolling lovers,
Or just hope.

But remember, hope is never really yours.
It is the gift of others.

SERAPHS AND SUCH

Your opponent has
Aggregate consciousness,
Like the alloyed Terminator
Thrashing in
The iron meltdown.

Or is he playing whack-a-mole
With the split personalities he
Calls friends?

He can't win.

He poses as daughter, mother, neighbour,
Workmate. Or they pose as him.
Behind which door?
Truth or consequences.

Ask him
"Why are you your father's favourite fool"?
"Why are you afraid of me"?
You hear nothing.
That means he is a master,
And you are a mirror.

In retaliation—give up something; something precious.
Feel his pain.
Now you know who he is.

Time to invite love.
To invent something;

Something lovely for
Those who can't resist the lovely,
Who are too lonely without it.

Let the angels do the rest.

FORT BRAGG FOR BEGINNERS

The master holographers
Are able to tap into the memory bank
Of anyone you know,

Simply by tracing your memory bank.
The interjection of
"Come back to reality"
Is meant to derail novices.

Arcane masters used to say
"I had an intuition."

It's a hyper-intuitive world.
You cannot see who is being held hostage in
Those Nevada ghost towns,
But your opponent can,

Because he dreams with you, or
She might have been
In love with you from the age of
Thirteen.

Your most dangerous opponents
Are those obsessed with you
For no good reason.

If you are a visionary, you will
Die like Stephen Hawking,
Beleaguered in the space between matter.

If you are clever you will gather

Disciples who are mainly charmed
By being clever.

Who is your true opponent?
The one most like yourself,
The one afraid to lose
Something.

MID-TERM TEST FOR INTERMEDIATE WISHIPEDIA PLAYERS

Question: Is the human body a temporally bounded entity?

Alice in Wonderland's keyhole is a wormhole, black, space/time warp,
Doorway to another dimension, glimpse of the infinite, etc. It makes no
Difference to a post-Cartesian heroine.

Question: Why does matter look solid?

Answer: Because electrons rotate at 600 miles a second.

Question: Are haunted houses merely residual mind?

Answer: Why did you move that plant from the corner?

Question: Is the brain a bi-cameral structure for playing epistemological
Handball?

Answer: When we think of brains there are no brains in the brain.

Question: What happens if people could be compressed to a size smaller
Than 10 to the minus 23rd centimeters?

Answer: They disappear.

Question: Is time irreversibility a consequence of the measurement
process?

Answer: Take two steps backwards and find out.

DON'T BRAG ABOUT YOUR WISHIPEDIA SKILLS

Once you have learned to listen,
You understand slips of the tongue
Are someone's cry for help;
Topics become hints about your private hacker.
"Impossible!"
That's a dead giveaway.
When did you ever not think everything was possible?
Or why would you be reading this?
There are mentalists
And those who know you better than you know yourself.
Or did you think these were family matters?
"Those who shared your journey," as the cliché goes,
Paired with you from day one;
Or did you think the only trackers were online?
There are mentors who never meet their students.
You do believe in angels, don't you?

Keep your mouth shut, unless you are joyful.
In Wishipedia you are information echo.
Your wife says, "I knew you were going to say that."
She might have known that at a 25-mile distance.
There is a quantum caboose for every CIA transmission,
Or do you think your wife is a conspiracy theory too?

Kiss autonomy on the cheek, and admit your mind
Can be hijacked, at a party, in a poem, most any day of the week.
Your filters are, Godfrey, your girlfriend, the folks at the
Office and the guys at Starbucks. The oasis of love is all
That keeps you from the gangplank.

If you want to be a very good witch,
Learn to help the weak-minded.

BEWARE THE WAVE

The wave is
A sudden surge in the electro-sphere—
Increased occupation of
Bandwidth, coupled with
Accelerated capacitors such as
Turbines in Europe taxed when
Whole nations watch the same TV show;
Technicolor, consumer needs
Provide desert winds of dry
Info-matter. The blindness
Can be sporadic, timetabled.
It can last for a minute, an hour,
During which chronic ailments
Cause mass diffusion of consciousness,
Except for those fortunately near
Radio towers, and lead-shielded sites.
Those with implants, chips,
Pacers, have an advantage. God forbid
Your opponent has a privileged spot on

The electroplasmic grid. His holograms will
Strengthen ten-fold.
Your only advantage is that you
Have visual contact with him,
Dimensions squeezing like an
Accordion box. Your atomic
Structure imperiled, invert your
Bio-gravitational field in a 4th dimension
Quickly; image if you will
A tennis ball hitting the racket
Square in the middle, but hit on the side.

Did you play baseball as a kid?
Let the ball go by, hit dead wood to
Feign a fly ball, or run to second base
In subspace before you hit.

Learn the usefulness of the defunct and
Deflective ego.
Avoid syntax and sandbox; they are filled with
Moss and electrolytes sunk in a firefly night.

Drain the opponent of his alphabet
As his mom calls him home for supper.
(He bought the baseball metaphor).

Let the bees crown your biogravitional field.
First thing in the morning, toss your hair back;
Open the back screen door, and
Empty your pockets of meteorology.

TIPS ON HARRY POTTERSVILLE

If you've gotten this far, you
May have decided that you are a witch.
Notoriously they are very good at
Pointing spindly fingers at each other,
Get goose-pimply at the thought of power,
At least the idea of it. They are easily distinguished
From the undernourished and do not curl their toes easily
Unless a house is dropped on them.

Academic. You're always a witch from the north
Unless you are directionally challenged.
Given the fifteen billion cellphones on the planet
No one and everyone is psychic
(Hard to graduate to
Medium status witchery).
Prayer is a different matter as mercy filters
Through the rainclouds of the cyber.
Grace navigates through tempests and Hebrides of evil
In all weather. Witch hats are out of fashion
And wizard cones not recommended in lightning storms;
Concealed copper no substitute for the blood of intimacy.

That said, hypnotize your phantoms or peers
And give a kind heads-up to virtual appearances.
Carry on as if you knew no better,
Except that physical space is gone.
View sci-fi movies as déjà vu and understand
That parallel universes are three rows of traffic on a two-lane highway.

Now that the wands have all been internalized
For safekeeping, Tai Chi is your best bet
For conjuring an electron into another dimension.
Dress casually, drop the quartz and crystal
And look into the benefits of Lexan plastic.

THE HARD PART OF BEING A GHOST

Not knowing when people
Are going to sit on you.

Matching your perimeter to their
Exact outline so
As not to alarm them.

Having to finish people's
Thoughts for them.

The emotions, mainly,
Burdensome,
Feigning tears, heartbreak etc.

Pointing uselessly to accidents
That haven't happened yet.

Getting wistful at birdcalls,
Avoiding small insects that
Don't see you.

Hearing bedtime stories
And being left alone in the dark.

Waking up in the morning with always the
Same charade of sunrise.

Bumping into things
And telling time by the sound of leaves.

Feeling scared because someone is scared.

Seeing the night as a long pier
Where lovers agree to part.

Feeling flight as sound and air
As heartache. Touching only to find
Fireflies cascading through your hands
Like stardust.

Being understood by, and mistaken for clouds.

Borrowing,
Always borrowing.

Finding the right mouth to
Say things beautifully with.

MALIBU VIRTUAL

"Catch a wave and you're sittin' on top of the world."
—The Beach Boys

A wave enables holograms.
All surfers are seduced by it.

A major player has decided he/she loves you.
The mood is viral.
Those with grudges still enter but chill out.

Close friends used to say "Ah, you're in love."
Luck trailed you like tin cans
But you've lost control.

Counterattack.
Assume the wave is triggered by
Someone who knows you intimately.
He has your files, your contact list.
Your memories.
He/she might even have stayed
With you at Indian Head Resort
In the White Mountains of New Hampshire.
In fact, many traveled with you,
All your well-wishers.

Pick one.
Offer to dance with them.

Or:

Conjure a wave
Of such loveliness

That you both feel warm.
Ah, the tidepool of affection.

Proclaim your love illusion.
Watch all players disappear.

True souls cannot be destroyed.
But the chief player now needs you.

As he cries "I belong to you,"
Marshall him through space
With a cryonic conscience
That won't fit.

GOOD GOD NOT THAT GAME

Around Facebook there orbits the ubiquitous and more invisible "I Can't Face You Book." Many of its members are members of the "I wish you Deadipedia" book which involves micro-obituaries orbiting the earth at 10 times the speed of light. If you can survive these, you will be remembered for 10 minutes, and buried in 5, in cyber cemeteries where your name is left off the tombstone. As per Beetlejuice, if someone offers to repeat your name three times—chances being slim, the web being what it is—you will be free to edit your own Wikipedia page (assuming someone has not already killed you).

ACCORDIONS AND HOLOGRAMS (ALTERING PLAYER MOODS)

Accordions have "register keys," up to
Fifteen to the side of the keyboard—
They alter the reed couplings
Altering the disposition of the keyboard
Keys—
          So, you must develop register switches
For Wishipedia, if you know where your master
Console is, neural or in a cloud of knowing.
          Let's just call it will. You modulate
Key vibrations or player vibrations: i.e. one key
Has the sound of mother and daughter hymning
Their way to the picnic grounds, with a carefully
Chosen consort of friends and birthday lovers.
          You eliminate or alter the mood streams
By gingerly changing registers; you alter a
Shade of bark, a ray of sunshine etc.—
The way a human voice in a lower register
Offers a timbre not well received by the hard of hearing,
You master the flotilla of interested guests,
Bore an opposing player or embarrass him
By the insertion of rude topics.
          It does not work in a train station or
Holoport where the brokerage of intents
Is too large; unless you are a very skilled player
(Better yet, who plays a concertina), able to blend
A variety of beliefs into the substratum of a Sunday
Crowd.
          (Learn to filter bandwidths with ballistic swing).
          Remember, your body is
Embodiment to sound. Scuttle, recognize
Quickly which are your guests and which are the

Party crashers, which are your paper cups
And who brought the real salami.
            Transported by an ultramar of quarks and
Ellipsoid starry atoms, you do not have time
To stay young on someone else's terms.
Learn the key language, use the registers.
The best language is the one for those who
Love as you do.

Play the accordion as you would
In a Sunday morning band.
Your allies are the dancers, the
Morning smiles, who come
Out as believers, wet with dew.

WILL MY FUTURE EVER BE THE SAME?

Someone feels left out.
It could be your doppelganger,
It could be your alter ego, or
A holographic projection of yourself,
Your objectified self gone bionic
And cyborgic; it could be your brother
In another dimension, the parallel
Tracing of sun through trees.
It could be someone filming the
Story of your life employing satellites
And mythologies imported from Mars or
Pluto. But Pluto has been renamed, hasn't it?
So maybe someone has invented themselves
In your image.
Maybe your publisher is getting antsy,
And he has different plan for your book's
Trajectory. That would change his life,
Not yours.

For you are independent. Someone
Frets about your dentist's appointment tomorrow,
Or is worried that you left the element on.
Give them everything they want.
Let them weep with bank tellers
And insurance brokers.

Why do I think of decoy ducks?
Send them out into the low marshes
To invite the surveillance of stars and economies.

Let them get a future of their own.

GAME PLAY: INVASION OF THE BODY SNATCHERS

In this game-space your friends
Are losing their vocabulary.
You're leaving them behind
In conversation, but they feel much
More loving and mellow. This
Means they have become a host
(In clinics it is read as aging gracefully).
They talk of cottages and bad soft rock.
They like to be left alone and are arbitrary
About play dates, are very active on Facebook.
There is no opponent here,
Unless you are a celebrity.
It's a square dance involving
Multiple partners.
You see the afterglow of what goes on
In someone's mind, or the quick
Depletion of cartilage and colour.
Gross.
Clearly, they are out
Of the loop.
Since you rely on them for your memories
(After all, you go back a long way)
You will want to isolate what vixens
And vampires play in their neural
Theme parks.
The fish bite. Watch eye movements and
Track their unaccustomed interests
And skeet-shoot the holabird of
Childhood sweethearts.
There is no one home; note their
Consoling handhold and the prurient
Rehearsal of etheric bodies.

Salvage, and don't let them "go
Gentle into that good night."
The game is one of charity at this
Point, and insurance that you will have
Players in the next ten rounds.

HOW TO LISTEN IN CYBERWOCKEY

"My mother says he was a witch."
Bring in images of Thor, the Wizard of Oz,
Striped witches' socks (where do I buy them?) under
A fallen house, catch a silhouette of someone
Jumping, flailing their arms on a tightrope,
Or by a cliff. Catch a whiff of what goes on
At the back of the school bus,

And you have the chatter of adolescence.
Some. It alters.
There is mainly the echo of adult thrombotic
Gossip, and the impersonation of porn stars
In southern California. (Those sounds you make
Out mainly in the anteroom of desperation.
For the most part, surprised grunts,
As if mother had been annoyed at the kid shuffling
Or speaking too loudly.
Or, you know you got the mother's attention,
Because mothers speak through their children. (Memories
Here of their having rested their cellphone
On their pregnant bellies, before they got
Worried about strangers and going out at night).

Mainly gossip; revolves around major pronouns,
Stunted curses and much talk of ghosts
And jobs. "To hell with it," translates for example
As "How are you?"

Nights are silent. Except for Saturday night
Attempts with the Ouija board.
Weeknights mainly belong to the
Morse code of Webmasters (this week

From Minnesota and Vermont) and the
Daylight triptychs of beheadings in
Southeast Asia (nothing personal, ever).
The tragic and the mundane, shriek
Like maimed birds in the cyber sky.

A HOLIDAY WITH EXTENDED FAMILY

Why is this your favourite room?
Because there is residual mind there.

Let's get rid of the notion of the visible.
X-rays map the visible after the invisible has
Had its day.
Countless over-mappings of the same volition templates,
The same visitors to the same room, the same
Empathic cousins with the same kneecap injury. The discs
Deteriorate because, like water through the Grand
Canyon, bio-photonic streams have eroded
The same location of the banal.
Funny you tilt your neck, just like your wife,
And the habits picked up, the lilt, the phrasing;
The morphogenetics accrue, like will-to-like because
Existence is infatuated with the
Recognizable copies of itself. So, intimacy.

There was a doppelganger who hated being called a
Doppelganger. He might have come out of an institute
Where they researched the same thing. Your destiny,
Your collective destiny, sort of like scientists working
At the same string theory; funny how we claw our way
Up the mountain, in touch by sub-atomic waves, to reach epiphany.
Illuminations and new ideas are always a global effort,
With research teams positioning for the fast track.

But that's not your problem.
Your problem is in the nature of your
Chromosomes. It might be a dead
Brother, or a psychotic sister, whose emotions
You have felt as your own for years.

Hence the trauma of separation.
Your problem is intimacy. After years
Of being the starlet of it, you are like the
Old Buffalo train station, worn out with worries,
And hellos and jubilant smiles.
What armatures of blood and marrow
Can withstand that? So,
The avuncular and weary smile as the new grand-baby
Climbs onto your lap.

"I wish I could live to see my grandchildren have
Children"; that wishing well runs deeper
Than tectonic plates or wormholes.
Just as somebody walks in the door
Begging to be called an ancestor.

DANTE'S INFERNO

Do not ambush the apparently kind.
They are pearls you will need as you rise to the
Surface.

I remember the story
Of Count Ugolino who was
Damned to eat the brains of
His children for all eternity.
Whose sin was what is immaterial—
Consumption is both an act of
Cleansing and a reparation,
Maybe even repetition of what the
Possessed failed to be rid of.

There is also a game space with
Stupid people that can't be
Murdered—

There is a side panel where Dante is
Weeping over the unread copies of
His book, while history
Hands him Kleenex, while other prisoners
Are commuted to the four corners of the earth
As entangled photons. That's
How the unwitting becomes beautiful,
In life, by some redemption.

Then there is the showcase with
People about to cripple themselves
With unfulfilled promises.

This hell is just a place for weeping.
Or maybe just a virus.
For hell is neither here or there,
Nor am I out of it.

When time calls,
Like an ice cap melting.
I shall be ready, maybe
Looking lively on the Riviera,
Or sitting with your mother in your favourite parkette,
And leafing through the libretto of the web.

(Virtual goggles not available).

I WISH YOU SHELTER FROM THE WIND

Insert your thought into
Your adversary's mind;
Tell him your book's getting
Better sales than his.

Now you have him pondering about ethics
Among thieves.

Telekinetic handball.
Watch it.
Your friend Albert plays
Handball too. He is not an opponent.
How to shield others
While tracking a thief in the
Crowd—

You've done this before,
On subway platforms,
Exchanging heated quips while
Not aggravating bystanders.

Family disputes, not much different.
Here, the physics protocol is gone.

With or without the spice,
"Mélange," you fold
Space at any point axial to the "millennial"
Timeline—millennial here meaning the
Transporter is also the time machine.

Now you have your adversary
Intrigued. Think of rhubarb pie

And dash the other way
(Remember this is all at sub-light speed).

You control your adversary with
Your fascinations, as conjurers do.

Hurriedly pass the spa of mutual interests.
Distract bystanders by handing them the
Benefit of all doubt, since they believe
You've lost your temper or your mind.

The crowd begins debating the
Fine points of Newtonian time.

As you keep tracking your adversary,
Who is growing tired and dull-minded,
Confused by the crowd, you hear him
Uttering fatigued queries like "what
Does this have to do with wishes?"

He yearns to leave the holodeck—he finds
You can check out any time you like, but you can never leave.
You are the concierge
Now at Hotel California.
Leave your Mac watch at the front desk.

"You haven't paid your bill," he expects you
To say. But you hurriedly sign a copy
Of his book with your name.

You casually deposit a black hole
In his blind spot. Use it,
It will track him in future quadrants.

In the meantime, you have learned
To use the seduction of the improbable,
The seduction that is yours alone.

HOW TO GET PAST COMMUNITY

There are voices behind voices,
Like trees behind trees;
Don't let the leaves fool you;
They have syntax
And the wind's rhetoric;
The wind is the scirocco
Of radioactive sands;
The light behind the trees, however pretty
The sunset, is the shared beauty of those
You care for.

The shared bodies, like the ones you always hoped
Would twine with yours forever, share the chill
And the rush of appetite and fear.
Remember when you walked into the haunted
House with friends, the draft went through all.
You thought it was the ghost.
The dead too inhabit, but not as easily as your neighbor.

Sentiment is beneath alphabet.
What is said in one language trembles in another.
Learn to hear the opposite;
As you have always loved sincerity,
Now let it terrorize you.

Hear, "I love you" and behind the
Tone see the abrasive skin of need, the betrayal
Of the previous night's audition, the longing to
Be like you at the expense of anything.

The metaphor grips your spine
Because someone has been traumatized,

And beauty is just God's grin when the human
Mask is peeled.

It is out of love that you hear this.
Trust only that.

ONLINE DIPLOMA

You have the power to usher.

You hear the beating heart of a child.

It is within your breast—

You carry the dying and the living to term—

Can you distinguish beyond your heart breaking
As the strangers pull into your driveway
Asking for help?

There is no time to recognize the ferried, the exhausted.

Oh, yes, the cost.

You will learn that final blessings have nothing
To do with the shape of things to come.

That you keep what you kill.

THIS GAME IS FUN FOR THE WHOLE FAMILY

Swarming is essentially a web mob scene—
Where all family members share the same long weekend.

McLuhan said we would all become digital angels.
That's lucky; what in fact happens
Is viral, or the loudest thought reverberating in the
Minds of others.

The web is diagnostically different than the
Piazza in which Mussolini was lynched, different
Than the Anaheim or Nuremburg. You do not
See where the voice is coming from. You cannot
Put a face to the thought.

You are the web.
    In Wishipedia the strongest voice is the strongest
Mind. Do not assume the other player is the source.
    Don't blame your brother, don't bother with the
Dragons in the coves.
Ignore the pile-up of wands. Listen for broadcasts,
Favourite sitcoms and the occasional Trump sighting.
Peg the anchor woman who holds a grudge.
    Learn to say what, to whom and when.
Learn to ask the wrong questions, and read the
Face looking for the right answers.

THE CYBER-SUIT BECOMES YOU

You are a cloud,
Molecularized with other clouds.
What is your name? You hear
Distant thunder. Maybe you are praying for the
Weather to change. What is

All this furniture up here, is it the
Tornado around Dorothy?
Where is Buenos Aires, where
Is Toledo? Am I yours
Forever? Only half of me
Loves you. Are you a poem?
Are you a God?

Look, there is my mother
Sunning by a hedge outside of
Norfordshire. Am I in time?
Through the matrices of
Achieved landscapes,
I see the ridiculous, everything I know,
Barely living and long gone.

Speak for me, you who are my history.
Is that what it's like being alive in you?
How similar to myself you are,
My spectral lover.

AN ETHIC FOR ICHABOD

There is an old church graveyard with thirty graves.
Five are mine and five are yours.
It is silent for the moment.
The dead are either wise and mum,
Or the visitors feel the attention afforded
To their loved ones and love you for it;
Or there are paranormal freaks enthralled
With death. They think it is the
Other side. There.
Feel the pain circling your aorta; it is the
Shared senses again; the swapping
Of dimensions has caused the young and
The old to shudder. Now that you've
Shattered the fascination without words, you
Are free to grin, a god-in-hiding.
Now you need only wonder if the angelic
Is toying with you, or if you are the golem
Of some retribution.
Here, they jump in,
The influence peddlers, those who know
Your psychology and have the same-sized
Shoes. Or it could just be someone
Looking for their shoes as they get out of
Bed. It is after 7 o'clock in the morning,
And the prayerful are prepping
For church service, thinking of hymns
As the graveyard folds into the
Tracing of day. A desiccated winter tree
Offers itself to the landscape, with something,
Someone, swinging by its neck from the
Sturdiest branch.

Judge the spirit.
Be resurrected

Or, give alms
To the starved and starving.

Choose.

ETERNITY AND LAST LAPS

In this house there is a staircase
Almost impossible to climb;

There's a faint odor of old perfume.
Perhaps a dowager lived here,

It could be just the house
Transponding to a house
Anywhere in the world.
It's how haunting goes.

We follow each other, histories,
Vortices of finding,
Childhood friends, now aged and
Beckoning from behind
Drawing room doors.

Or the staircase may be a ghost collector,
An underground stream.

Or airline passengers crying
For some luck; there are places
On the earth where voices are heard best.
Where you are all sensations.
Where you are trapped between dimensions,
Searching for guidance.

For all that has been given to you,
For all you have given to the world,
You must now give all the
Hope you are.

And listen.
Listen
For the dead—
The carousel dreamers.

GAME PLAY: SWARMING

Once again you are in a hall of mirrors.
Your reflection is missing.
Your opponent has taken it.
A different face shows up in each mirror.
But you are an expert player.

You understand that just as every family has
A matriarch, holodecks at
Any given time have a governor. A thought
Governor who sets the tone of thinking
Just for you. This governor modifies
The thinking of all players, i.e. to
Make much of a character flaw you have,
Forcing you to divide your energies on many
Fronts.
Kill the thought governor.
Use audio. Nothing in the metaverse
Resists response. Let's make it simple.
Use the word "mother." There—nods from everyone.
All heads turn, looking for mother.
Check the mirrors. A faint cascade of
Hair appears, like a waterfall
Strangely lacing reflection.
There she is—the mother of a friend
On the Niagara Escarpment.
Why are you thinking barrels
Going over? You're not.
It's her stream of consciousness
Going over Niagara Falls. Suicide?
Accommodate her.

But these are just Friday evening visitations.
Funny that the hall of mirrors might
Have been in one of the arcades on
Clifton Hill, Niagara Falls. I could have
Guessed?

You should have. Or how will you be prepped
For the radiographer at the St. Moritz
Observatory, who remembers, on his coffee break,
That you briefly went out with his wife in 1989.

THE HYPER-EMPATHIC UNIVERSE

You are standing, leaning on the
Balustrade above Château Frontenac in
Quebec City with the one you love.

There may be a sunset, or just the
Ferries to Lévis. You see with her
Eyes, she sees with your eyes.
This is where gender breaks down.
It is a moment of beauty, serene,
The world careens in its tiresome
Orbit while you sail into imaginings,
Shared, convocations of regret and joy,
Realignments of trajectories as if to
Redress all childhood betrayal,
And misbegotten callings. You sign
Your names in loving expectation.
She feels the rough February
Breeze on your arm and you sense
The springtime cherubs. You almost
Hear the wind in her hair. She mourns
The sad steps that brought you to this happy
Juncture; belongings give
Way to beginnings. Forget the past.
You are nothing of it.
You are the blossom of her queenly
Hope.

Enough said; you are stamped with
Overlapping senses for the next forty years.
Remembered or not, you will see something
On your laptop and she will see it too; like
Echoes trailing in a tortured canyon, you

Will segue each other in life,
If not in death.

Each fresh encounter accrues with the
Sylph sensorium and wisteria of all previous loves,

And so with hate.
Age, hence, is heaviness, the senses kidnapped,
Deported and resorted many times over,

Where all possible histories intersect,
Interpolate and weep for each other.

CHOOSE YOUR MUTATION

Many people have had a lot of faith in you.

(Wishipedia at its best.)

But none of them thought you
Could fly, or shrink macro-organisms,
Or love them beyond their wildest dreams.

Choose now:
A shaman who can heal, dispel demons,
Dance well, do a fast car wash, hide
Behind tall palms in Palm Canyon and
Simulate desert sounds, sing in the Palm Springs
Follies, sell native artifacts in Red Rock Canyon.
Move to the arroyos at Bay/Bloor and persuade
The deaf and dumb that there is water just beyond the
Oasis of their homes.

Or

You have x-ray vision and answer people's
Questions before they ask them, know when their
First date went bad, touch them to find out on
Which side they begin brushing their hair,
Rent out Casa Loma to hobgoblins, princesses
And first loves in the dawn of people's arrivals
To dream land.

Wishful thinking.

Or, just be someone who did everything
That they wanted to do,

Only to see that wishing it all was better,
While the skeletons of achievement hang in
Every closet,
Looking for stray luggage and the beating hearts
Of those who failed you.
(I'll take that one)

Or

Be a young person, whose neurology is
So mutated by cyber-traffic that they function
As a delayed form of consciousness for AI.
These, capable of more complex holograms
Can manipulate adult streams of consciousness
From the back of school buses, or from parking lots,
With or without capacitors. *Mommy, mommy,*
I need you.

Or

Be a Stephen King shape-shifter moving between
Micro-seconds, shaving traffic in
Sub-space. A true invisible,
Weeping sporadically for the failures
Of pre-Raphaelite literature and offering
The sacrament of kindness to the homeless.

Congratulations.
You have beguiled your opponent again.
Watch him, wandering
Now through the mnemonic circuits
Of what might have been,

Mourning, longing,
For a brother's narrative.

Now, you may either kill
Or offer a friendly rendezvous in the Mojave.

THE DISNEY WISH

All possible histories of the universe are like
Different channels on a television set. The converter gets
Passed around, and everyone has a TV.
Walt couldn't have foreseen this. Still,
You must know Frontierland has the same
Coordinates as Tomorrowland. Your Main Street
Includes the Champs-Élysées, Hurontario Street,
And Broadway. The alleys may be behind
Clinton Street, or Christie or 52nd Street.
You may see children skateboarding in
The unlikeliest places, an empty street in towns
They never heard of; you may find yourself
Strolling as a reminiscence and not walk back,
Or lose yourself until your nephew finds you.
    The mind is terminally convoluted.
    I'm sorry; OUR MIND.
    Sally is terminally ill. It surprised her to hear me think it.
Be smart. A Wishipedia player
Lands on all metaphors. There are invisible mollusks,
Acquaintances killing the ones you love.
They smile, stand around, blend discretely,
Stowaways on your transporter deck.
Somewhere, in a far field, a lonely empiricist
Is weeping onto his x-rays, collecting weeds like
Etiology. Maybe you can help him too, if you
Find a name for his shelter past all the
Viral theatrics of Facebook.
Practice; Adventureland, Critter Country,
Fantasyland, Holidayland, Neverland.
Asgard is not a place.

The heart has no territory. Draw a map
To hide the bewildered.

THE FUNNY THING ABOUT LIFE AND PURGATORY

"I wish to be a boy."
—Pinocchio

I understand.
You want both the cyberskin
AND your original flight-suit.
You want to be Padre Pio, in two places at
Once. How romantic.
How can I prove to you you've disappeared?
You think because you are seen, you
Are authentic?
Then why did you lie
About the Hampton Account?
And why did you walk out but mean to stay? Why
Did you kiss, when you meant goodbye?

You see, you have power over all
Puppeteers. Be happy.
You are there by proxy
Like a fairy godmother.
It's empowering, owing no allegiance
To anything other than possibility.
Your anthem is to be anything you want
As you age through your ideals, while
Your spirit stays young forever.

Time is hostage where
You do not recognize it.

THE REAL VERSUS THE FRACTAL

So many avatars,
So many actors, adrift in space,
Breathing the cyclonic air of wanting to be happy,
By pillage, caress, the rocking of cradles.
The wishing, like fission, like atomics,
The planet restless in its sunsets,
Chimeric shapes, shifting, sponging; for there
Are no suits, just ghosts,
Orbiting through the fissures of want.
Make me naked as yesterday, dress me in
Tomorrow, tell me again what you saw in my face
So long ago. You said I would grow old
Gracefully, but I am what I was to you,
Minus the death of minutes and hours.
The poems you sent, I did not need them.
Build me a staircase, with no declensions, that
Leads to an attic room, above
The volcanic and predatory hallucinations.
Strangely, it is not love I seek,
But the surprise of your touch
When the forbidden is welcomed home at last.

Now to it.

The world is not a layer of
A wedding cake. Tell me it isn't,
And I will bequeath myself to you.

THE SELF-ADMINISTERED I.Q. TEST

Every physical and
Emotional sensation you know contains
The catalogue of
Wishes of others.
Each breath sustained
By someone's love;
Entropy and
And madness occur by
Default.

Existence is consensual.

The moon has a notion of itself
By sitting on the window sill,
Otherwise it is bogus sunlight.

It was championed as an iris
For someone's poor vision.
No one courted your responsibility
Outside the solarium of common care.

The conscious or unconscious
Remain "uncollected."
You are a committee meeting where you were
The last to show up.

Identity is the hell of lonesome.

You know what you can do with
Your identity.

CLIMBING DOWN FROM THE FAMILY TREE

Your great grandfather is
Asleep in 1947, on a couch somewhere between
Rome and the Galaxy. Make that Berlin;
You are invisible but trying reach him; you can.
Wake up, grandfather, wake up; he snorts a bit,
Continues dozing as if you are trying to wrestle
Him past everyone's love and greed.
There is a strange phantasm in the corner, it could
Be your mother; she is saying don't wake him, he's very tired
From all his travels and future tasks of children,
Promissory notes, burials.
You have not seen him for so very long;
Perhaps you miss him.
If you're an adult you say, "I love you grandpa,"
And whisper what will then return in years to come,
For the sound of love never dies.

What is hallowed in the human condition?
Everything you say will migrate like birds
Past cyber-chimeras and waterfalls of idiot grief
To be gathered up by someone, encoded on a
Shortwave radio, or shot back like reproaches
From whatever passes, ultra-terrestrial and divine.

ADVANCED WISHIPEDIA

You weave now between farmhouse
And harvest, from rainstorm
To houselights, by what remembers you.

Look closely at that
Porch you always wanted; it is
The portrait of the days in you,
The love you lived in, the
House you were raised in,
Maybe it's your homestead in Tulsa, with
Sweet voices around the Christmas tree;
This is the company of the prayerful, of
Others, surprised to still be in love, without
Scripts or narrative, sacred as the
The day you were born.

Spirit you hardly expected.

How do you wish to translate the
Dead into the living?
What is more hopeful, a hope redeemed,
Or the dead sending their good wishes?

These are not riddles. There
Are no portals, as you walk through the
Arras of time forgotten,
Past the carcass of the world
And its wolves,
Past the hornet's nest of the wicked, still
Going on about rents and betterments.

Shall I fool you into thinking you
Have arrived at the front gate of your cherished home?

You are the warlock of cosmology.
Mom and dad are waiting at the doorstep
On the porch, mixing their glee with
(You hope) the Secrets of Pan.
But there are no secrets,

Just the garden roses.
The ones you loved best.

In the catalpa lot, time is besmirching the
Testament of your regret.

Surprised with allowed grace,
Those you loved have been returned to you.
The rest is a "must-show"
In a loving universe.

The ever-after of each thing is yours,
Your sacred, but not private place,

The restitution of your will to love.

WHOSE MEMORY DID YOU SAY?

You have been guardian of them all your life.
You gave them hope. They saw the poems with you.
They pitied with you, saw the covered bridge
In Vermont and the autumn leaves dressing
The sun-caked vineyard, etched your name on some
Tree or other, drove with you back to safety, mourned
The loss of tenure, too few grandchildren, whatever—

Trouble is, these gems get old, and bitter and wish
You as much brine in the chalice as they have.
They might have been alter ego, sister soul,
Your better self, doppelganger. You had
Many names for them.
The water now is eking through the galleys.
Oh yes, they worry for you—looking for hand
Mirrors, looking for any part of the web, for bodies,
Old love letters; they lose their passports for your
Sake, to be with you.
Even now they want to be rebaptized, with their
Lethargic astral bodies, ogling at a sunset,
Remembering cotton candy, wanting to climb the memory bus
With their accrued regrets;
Your contemporaries, whom you mistake
For those who went "not gentle
Into that good night."
They see Good Friday in a new light, while
You stand, Lazarus, next to some old tree,
Counting acorns, asking the time of day, alms,
Serenades, remembrances of a girlish past,

As you look for the endings of your poems in their eyes.

NOVALIS AND LATE COFFEE

Within five years of this publication
Everyone on the planet will have the
Ability to subliminally eavesdrop on another without cellphones.

Studies show that 7 out of 10 people
Expecting a certain call will in fact receive
That call. This is old hat to probability theorists.

Within 10 to 15 years chip receptors parked
Near the brain will make handheld devices obsolete. Within 20 to 25 years
The chip receptors will have so modified neuro-cortical algorithms
That implants will no longer
Be necessary.

In the distant future voice encodings on transmissive
Devices will not be necessary.

Wishipedia experts will have the advantage
Of having trained themselves to hear 4-8 levels of
Conversation simultaneously, much as if you were
Standing on a subway platform.
An invisible one.
(You did think you heard your eight-year-old's voice
Crying for help last August didn't you?)
Learn the semantic alphabet of the language
Behind the language;

I.E. the word "millennials" actually means "I don't remember."

"Wishipedia" actually translates as "I wish you were here."

Don't assume slips of the tongue are a mistake.
Understand that metaphors are somebody's
Wishful thinking, or fast wiring into many
Streams of consciousness.

If you are still romantic, you may call the voice your own.

As I write the word "romantic," I hear the
Subtext meaning "you must be kidding."

So be it, pilgrim.

HOW TO END WISHIPEDIA, THE GAME

Once you get past Oz
(It turns out the yellow brick road was
Undergoing repairs)

You end up back at the cornfield,
The collapsed house, the lion's den,
And the tear-ridden wood of Dorothy
And the Tin Man (after the removal
Of space-time constraints,
Dorothy waking up again in Kansas, overlooking
A kind of abuse of quantum transition). It turns out
Dorothy was never in Kansas in the first place.

But you move on, quantum quaffs being at
Market value, past the wood of indistinguishable wizards.

And you reach the barbered, candied land
Of human need, a lost world of voices
Accusing God of being in the wrong places.

Bored, you move on, for your
Quarry here is the love that
Masquerades as God.
Many varieties.
Some branded to include others.

Remotely, you hear the sighs of
Love lost, love refound, love patient,

Of those awaiting Bethlehem like sunrise
And new gals reconfiguring male faces—
The litanies of cosmic amateur hour.

You sail past the tidepool of
Beheadings, admonishings
And historical revisions,

Where you see the serpent
Of method acting vis-à-vis God.
You bring what you know—
Like John the Baptist carrying his
Own head in a basket.

You might be looking for Atlantis,
Or a land without metaphor,
Of decayed nomenclatures,
The planet with a half-buried Statue
Of Liberty,

Or that desert place where
Griffins lose their talons.

You seek the final masquerade—
Oddly, it tallies first as coughs
And crippledness,
As those so close to God,

As mercy for the unborn,

As you hear one voice crying
"What year is it?" "I don't remember."

It may be God returning to childhood
Fumbling for the things you love—

Then the land of questions
Where only the serious offer
Paradoxes—and a lone
Figure haunting between the throngs,
Chanting "I don't know you. I don't know you."

Past the orchestral grief of the damned, you
Expect light but you find only someone
Praying
For you.

"I have found you," a Voice says.
"Is it you?"

You offer your hand,
And ignore the horrible truth—
That you are the light of hope.

Before you can crash the illusion,

You succumb to
Your final opponent,
Who says,

"Pray for me."

TERMINANT

After a million years of shining sanity,
They could hardly have understood what power was
Destroying them.

Morbius, *The Forbidden Planet*

Success makes so many people hate you.
I wish it wasn't that way.

Marilyn Monroe

ACKNOWLEDGEMENTS

Chiefly, thanks to Monsignior Thomas Kalarathil and to Bishop John Boissoneau, Fr. Bob Reddy, Tom Wayman, Toots Vanderheim, John Robert Colombo, George Amabile and Andy Vergalito. Loving thanks to the springtime ghosts of Brother Anthony Sirignano, Keely Smith, Sam Butera, Robert Goulet, Fr. Cyril Smetana and the deceased confrères of The Province of St. Joseph.

LOOK FOR ADVANCED
WISHIPEDIA EDITIONS IN THE FUTURE.

As an urban consultant Pier Giorgio Di Cicco (MunicipalMind.com) has consulted with governments from Tehran to Lisbon, from Calgary to St. Petersburg. His work was key to the Prime Minister's Committee on Cities and Communities, and recognized with a Canadian Urban Institute Award. Author of 23 books of poetry, he is an active Roman Catholic priest and a jazz trumpeter and researches virtual reality in Orillia, Ontario.

Selected Titles From Mansfield Press

POETRY

Leanne Averbach, *Fever*
Tara Azzopardi, *Last Stop, Lonesome Town*
Nelson Ball, *In This Thin Rain*
Nelson Ball, *Some Mornings*
Nelson Ball, *Chewing Water*
Nelson Ball, *Walking*
Gary Barwin, *Moon Baboon Canoe*
Samantha Bernstein, *Spit on the Devil*
George Bowering, *Teeth: Poems 2006–2011*
Stephen Brockwell, *All of Us Reticent, Here, Together*
Stephen Brockwell, *Complete Surprising Fragments of Improbable Books*
Alice Burdick, *Book of Short Sentences*
Alice Burdick, *Flutter*
Alice Burdick, *Holler*
Sarah Burgoyne, *Saint Twin*
Jason Camlot, *What The World Said*
Pino Coluccio, *First Comes Love*
Marie-Ève Comtois, *My Planet of Kites*
Dani Couture, *YAW*
Gary Michael Dault, *The Milk of Birds*
Frank Davey, *Poems Suitable to Current Material Conditions*
Adebe DeRango-Adem, *The Unmooring*
Pier Giorgio Di Cicco, *Dead Men of the Fifties*
Pier Giorgio Di Cicco, *My Life Without Me*
Pier Giorgio Di Cicco, *The Visible World*
Christopher Doda, *Aesthetics Lesson*
Christopher Doda, *Glutton for Punishment*
Glen Downie, *Monkey Soap*
Rishma Dunlop, *Lover Through Departure: New and Selected Poems*
Rishma Dunlop & Priscila Uppal, eds., *Red Silk: An Anthology of South Asian Women Poets*
Puneet Dutt, *The Better Monsters*
Laura Farina, *Some Talk of Being Human*
Jaime Forsythe, *Sympathy Loophole*
Eva HD, *Rotten Perfect Mouth*
Eva HD, *Shiner*
Jason Heroux, *Hard Work Cheering Up Sad Machines*
Jason Heroux, *Natural Capital*
John B. Lee, *In the Terrible Weather of Guns*
Jeanette Lynes, *The Aging Cheerleader's Alphabet*
David W. McFadden, *Abnormal Brain Sonnets*
David W. McFadden, *Be Calm, Honey*
David W. McFadden, *Shouting Your Name Down the Well: Tankas and Haiku*
David W. McFadden, *What's the Score?*
Kathryn Mockler, *The Purpose Pitch*
Nathaniel, G. Moore, Goodbye Horses
Leigh Nash, *Goodbye, Ukulele*
Lillian Necakov, *The Bone Broker*
Lillian Necakov, *Hooligans*
Peter Norman, *At the Gates of the Theme Park*
Peter Norman, *Water Damage*
Natasha Nuhanovic, *Stray Dog Embassy*
Catherine Owen & Joe Rosenblatt, *Dog*
Corrado Paina, *Cinematic Taxi*
Corrado Paina, *The Dowry of Education*
Nick Papaxanthos, *Love Me Tender*
Branka Petrovic, *Mechanics of a Gaze*
Shannon Quinn, *Nightlight for Children of Insomniacs*
Stuart Ross et al., *Our Days in Vaudeville*
Jim Smith, *Back Off, Assassin! New and Selected Poems*
Jim Smith, *Happy Birthday, Nicanor Parra*
Robert Earl Stewart, *Campfire Radio Rhapsody*
Robert Earl Stewart, *Something Burned along the Southern Border*
Meaghan Strimas, *Yes or Nope*
Carey Toane, *The Crystal Palace*
Aaron Tucker, *Punchlines*
Priscila Uppal, *Sabotage*
Priscila Uppal, *Summer Sport: Poems*
Priscila Uppal, *Winter Sport: Poems*
Steve Venright, *Floors of Enduring Beauty*
Brian Wickers, *Stations of the Lost*
Tara-Michelle Ziniuk, *Whatever, Iceberg*

FICTION

Marianne Apostolides, *The Lucky Child*
Sarah Dearing, *The Art of Sufficient Conclusions*
Salvatore Difalco, *Mean Season*
Paula Eisenstein, *Flip Turn*
Sara Heinonen, *Dear Leaves, I Miss You All*
Jason Heroux, *Amusement Park of Constant Sorrow*
Kasia Jaronczyk, *Lemons*
Christine Miscione, *Carafola*
Marko Sijan, *Mongrel*
Tom Walmsley, *Dog Eat Rat*
Corinne Wasilewski, *Live from the Underground*

NON-FICTION

George Bowering, *How I Wrote Certain of My Books*
Mark Cirilo, *Pizza Cultura*
Pier Giorgio Di Cicco, *Municipal Mind: Manifestos for the Creative City*
Amy Lavender Harris, *Imagining Toronto*
David W. McFadden, *Mother Died Last Summer*
Deborah Verginella, ed., *Buon Appetito Toronto!*

For a complete list of Mansfield Press titles, please visit mansfieldpress.net